Helping Children See Jesus

ISBN: 978-1-64104-001-3

The Nature of Man
Old Testament Volume 3:
Genesis Part 3

Author: Arlene Piepgrass
Illustrator: Vernon Henkel
Computer Graphic Artist: Andrew Cross
Typesetting and Layout: Morgan Melton, Patricia Pope

© 2018 Bible Visuals International
PO Box 153, Akron, PA 17501-0153
Phone: (717) 859-1131
www.biblevisuals.org

All rights reserved. No part of this publication may be reproduced, stored in a retrieval system or transmitted in any form by any means, electronic, mechanical, photocopy, recording or otherwise, without the prior permission of the publisher, except as provided by USA copyright law.

RELATED ITEMS

To access related items (such as activities, memory verse posters and translated texts) please visit our web store at shop.biblevisuals.org and enter 2003 in the search box on the page.

FREE TEXT DOWNLOAD

To access a FREE printable copy of the teaching text (PDF format) in English or other available languages, enter S2003DL in the search box. Add the item to your cart, and use coupon code XTACSV17 at checkout. Once your order is processed you will receive an email with a link to the free download.

Lesson 1
JACOB: BORN WITH A SINFUL NATURE

NOTE TO THE TEACHER
Abraham was declared righteous because he believed God. This did not mean that Abraham never sinned. But God forgave Abraham because of his faith in God. Likewise, we who are Christian believers are justified by faith (Romans 5:1) and accepted in the Beloved (Jesus Christ). (See Ephesians 1:6.) Our sins are forgiven through His blood (Ephesians 1:7) and we are no longer under God's condemnation (Romans 8:1). However, this does not mean we will never sin again. Instead, like Paul (Romans 7:18-25), we continue to do things which we know are sin and which we do not want to do. We each have an old sin nature which daily wants its own way. Consequently, there is a constant battle within each heart. (See Galatians 5:17.) Help your students to understand this conflict.

Scripture to be studied: Genesis 24:1-67; 25:24-34; 27:1-46

The *aim* of the lesson: To show that Christian believers still have their old sin natures which disobey God.

What your students should *know*: That the heart is deceitful and desperately wicked (Jeremiah 17:9).

What your students should *feel*: A desire to obey God and let Him plan their lives.

What your students should *do*: Yield themselves each day to the One Who is able to give them victory over the old sin nature.

Lesson outline (for the teacher's and students' notebooks):
1. Jacob's parents (Genesis 24:67; 25:19-23).
2. Jacob's birth (Genesis 25:24-26).
3. Jacob's youth (Genesis 25:27-34).
4. Jacob's deceit (Genesis 27:1-33).

The verse to be memorized:
Walk in the Spirit, and ye shall not fulfil the lust of the flesh. (Galatians 5:16)

THE LESSON
1. JACOB'S PARENTS
Genesis 24:67; 25:19-23

Isaac was a living miracle. When he was born, his father, Abraham, was 100 years old. Sarah, his mother, was 90 years old. People that old do not have babies. So the birth of Isaac was indeed a miracle.

Growing up, Isaac learned that there is only *one* God: the living God, who created the world and everything in it. He learned, also, that there is only one way to be accepted by God. To have his sins forgiven he would have to offer the blood of an animal as a sacrifice.

Abraham also explained to Isaac that through their family all the nations of the earth would one day be blessed. The Son of God would come to earth through him.

When Isaac was about 40 years old, his father became concerned about getting him a wife. The Canaanites, among whom they lived, worshiped idols. They did not trust in the living God.

One day Abraham said to his oldest servant, "Eliezer, my son Isaac needs a wife. God has promised to bless all of the nations of earth through me and my family. Isaac must have a wife who will trust and worship the true and living God. Go to my homeland. Find the right wife for Isaac from among my people."

Eliezer had a question. "Suppose the girl will not come to this land to marry a man whom neither she nor her family has ever seen."

"Do not worry, Eliezer. The Lord God of Heaven who led me, will lead you. He will show you the right girl. He will make her willing to come."

Eliezer loaded expensive gifts on ten of Abraham's camels and, together with other servants, began the long journey.

When Eliezer got near Haran (where Abraham's relatives lived), he stopped by a well. "Lord God," he prayed, "please show me the girl You have chosen for Isaac. I will wait here by the well. When the girls come to water their animals I will ask them for a drink of water. Cause the girl of Your choice to give me a drink willingly. And have her get water for my camels also. You have chosen a wife for Isaac. Do not let me make a mistake. I want to take Your choice back for my master's son."

Show Illustration #1

Soon a beautiful girl named Rebekah came to the well. Eliezer asked, "Will you please give me a drink from your pitcher?"

"Yes, surely," Rebekah replied cheerfully. "And I will get water for your camels too."

"Who is your father?" Eliezer asked. "Would he give me a place to sleep tonight?"

Rebekah answered, "My father is Bethuel and my grandfather is Nahor. I know they would be happy to have you stay at our house. We can take care of your animals and servants too."

Nahor! That is Abraham's brother! Eliezer remembered. Then he prayed, "O, my God, thank You for answering my prayer. Thank You for leading me to my master's own family. Thank You for choosing such a lovely girl for Abraham's son. Please make her family willing to send her with me. Make her willing to go with me!"

And God did just that. It was indeed a happy day when Isaac and Rebekah met.

2. JACOB'S BIRTH
Genesis 25:24-26

Isaac and Rebekah were married 20 years. But they had no children. They had many servants. They had large flocks of animals and many tents. They were wealthy. But they longed for a baby.

Finally God told Rebekah, "You are going to have twin boys. The oldest is usually the spiritual leader of the family. But it will be different with your sons. The younger one is going to be the leader. The older one will serve the younger one."

The day came when the twins were born. The firstborn was named Esau. He was red and hairy. His brother's name was Jacob.

Show Illustration #2
Isaac's tent was full of joy because of those two boys! Both Isaac and Rebekah praised God for keeping His promise.

3. JACOB'S YOUTH
Genesis 25:27-34

When Esau became old enough, he loved to go hunting. But that was all Esau liked to do. He was not interested in knowing what God had planned for his life. He was too restless to be bothered. Esau simply lived for each day.

Jacob was not interested in hunting. He stayed close to the tents. His mother, Rebekah, told him about God's wonderful promises. "You are the one, Jacob, who will receive the birthright," she explained. "Esau is older. It should be his. But God said that you will have this blessing."

"Mother," Jacob asked, "what good is it to have the birthright?"

Show Illustration #3
(*Teacher:* When you mention the inheritance, point to the coins in the top of the illustration. Indicate the crown when speaking of the "head of our family." When referring to the Redeemer, show the cross (of Christ) piercing the serpent's head as foretold in Genesis 3:15. The seed of the woman (Christ) shall bruise the serpent's (Satan's) head. Satan was defeated when Christ died on the cross and rose from the dead.)

"My son, when your father dies you will inherit twice as much as Esau. (See Deuteronomy 21:17.) But more important, you will be head of our family. You will have the honor of being the spiritual leader. You will guide us in worshiping the true and living God." This, Rebekah knew. What she may not have understood was this: because of the birthright, Jacob would be the ancestor of the promised Redeemer–the One who would defeat Satan.

Jacob often thought about what his mother told him. *How will I ever get the birthright from Esau?* he wondered. *I have to think of some way.*

One day when Esau came home from hunting, he was exhausted and hungry. Jacob was fixing a pot of stew that smelled delicious.

"Jacob, I am so hungry I am going to die. Give me a bowl of your stew," he begged.

Jacob thought, *Here is my chance.* "Yes, sure. I will give you a bowl of stew, Esau, if you will give me your birthright."

"You can have it. What good is it to me anyway? If I die from hunger the birthright will mean nothing to me. Just give me the stew. My birthright is yours."

"You promise, Esau?" questioned Jacob, waiting to be certain that Esau would not go back on his word.

"I promise," replied Esau.

For one little bowl of stew, Esau traded all the rights of the oldest son. Thinking no more about it, he went his way.

4. JACOB'S DECEIT
Genesis 27:1-33

Years later their father, Isaac, was almost blind. One day Rebekah heard him in his tent talking to Esau.

"Listen, my son," Isaac said, "I am getting old. Soon I will die. Take your bow and arrows and get some venison. Prepare me some delicious meat to eat. Then I will give you the blessings which belong to you, my firstborn son."

"I shall go immediately," Esau replied.

When Rebekah heard this, she was terrified. She remembered that God had told her that Jacob, the younger, would receive the blessing which belonged to the oldest son. (See Genesis 25:23.) What should she do?

Quickly a scheme came to her mind. She called Jacob and told him what she had heard his father say. "Do exactly what I tell you, Jacob," she commanded. "Go out and kill two young goats. Bring them to me. I will fix your father's favorite dish for him. Then you will take it to him. After he has eaten, he will bless you. Hurry! You must get to your father first."

"But, Mother!" Jacob protested. "My hands and neck are smooth. Esau's are covered with hair. When my father touches me, he will know I have tried to fool him. Then, instead of blessing me, he will curse me."

"Leave that to me," Rebekah ordered. "Hurry and do what I said!"

Why would Rebekah plan to deceive her husband and older son? She had the sin nature with which she was born. Her sinful nature made it easy for her to forget God. It caused her to go her own way instead of God's way. (See Jeremiah 17:9.) Jacob was born with this same sin nature. And every child that comes into the world is born with a sinful nature. (See Romans 5:12.)

God had told Rebekah that His blessing would go to Jacob. She should have waited to see how God would work things out. But neither Rebekah nor Jacob thought about God. Instead, Rebekah gave Jacob Esau's best clothes to wear. She covered his hands and neck with goat skins to make him feel hairy like Esau. Jacob took the good-smelling meat and fresh baked bread and went into Isaac's tent. "Father, here I am," he announced.

"Who are you?" Isaac asked.

"I am your older son, Esau," Jacob lied. "Sit up and eat the venison I have prepared for you – and bless me."

"You are back so quickly," said his father, doubting it was really Esau.

"Yes, the Lord helped me find an animal," Jacob lied again. (It was getting easier to lie!)

Isaac ordered, "Come here, let me feel you! I want to be sure you are really Esau." He still doubted that it was his older son.

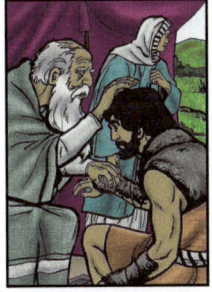

Show Illustration #4
Rubbing his hands over the goat hair on Jacob's hand and neck, Isaac shook his head. "Yes, it is Esau," he said. "Your voice sounds like Jacob's. But I can feel that you are Esau. Bring me the meat so I can eat it and bless you."

After eating, Isaac said, "Come here and kiss me, my son." Jacob obeyed and Isaac smelled his clothing, convinced finally that this really was Esau. Then Isaac prayed his blessing upon him. He asked God to make him prosperous. He added, "Be the master of your brother. May all your relatives bow down to you and serve you."

Jacob rushed out of the tent so Esau would not find him there. He just escaped in time! For right then, Esau came into the tent. "I'm here, Father," he said. I've fixed the meat exactly as you like it. Sit up and eat."

"Who are you?" Isaac cried.

"I'm your son Esau. I have done what you asked me to do."

Isaac shook all over. "If you are Esau, who was just in here? Whom did I bless?"

Realizing what had happened, Esau began to cry. Imagine a big, muscular hunter crying! "My brother's a cheater. First he cheated me out of my birthright. Now he has cheated me out of my father's blessing. I hate him! Oh, Father, bless me too!" he begged.

Isaac now realized that what he wanted for Esau was what God wanted for Jacob. "My son, you shall live by the sword. You will serve your brother. But the time will come when you will break his yoke from your neck."

Leaving the tent, Esau furiously determined to get even with Jacob. "I hate him! I am going to kill him!"

Do you think he succeeded? We will find out in our next lesson.

Our hearts are just as desperately wicked as Esau's, Jacob's, and Rebekah's. Christ, God's Son, died on the cross as punishment for our wicked sins. Do you believe that the Lord Jesus Christ is the Son of God? Do you believe He died for you? Have you asked Him to forgive your sins? Have you placed all your trust in Him? If so, you are a child of God.

But probably there are times when you get angry. You lie. You scheme to get your own way. That is sin. You do not want to sin. But you seem unable to help it. Why? Because you still have your sinful nature. God will forgive these wicked things when you confess them to Him and ask His forgiveness. (See 1 John 1:9.)

Let us thank God that the Lord Jesus, who had victory over Satan and sin, lives in our hearts. Ask Him to help you to live the way *He* wants you to live. Yield yourself right now and ask Him for victory over your old sinful nature.

Lesson 2
JACOB MADE AWARE OF HIS SINFUL NATURE

Scripture to be studied: Genesis 28; Scriptures mentioned in lesson.

The *aim* of the lesson: To show the need of salvation because of what we are by nature.

What your students should *know:* That God forgives sins only through His Son.

What your students should *feel:* A hatred for sin.

What your students should *do:* Trust Jesus Christ for forgiveness and a new nature.

Lesson outline (for the teacher's and students' notebooks):

1. Jacob's flight (Genesis 27:41–28:5).
2. Jacob's vision (Genesis 28:10-12).
3. God's promise (Genesis 28:13-15).
4. Jacob's vow (Genesis 28:18-22).

The verse to be memorized:

Walk in the Spirit, and ye shall not fulfil the lust of the flesh. (Galatians 5:16)

> **NOTE TO THE TEACHER**
>
> Jacob had parents who knew the Lord. Yet he himself had to place his personal trust in God. He had to receive God's pardon for sin. Sadly, there is no evidence that Jacob repented when he had the marvelous vision at Bethel. There was absolutely no change in his life until 20 years later when he returned to Bethel.
>
> Like Jacob, we deserve only punishment for sin. But we have the Lord's glorious promise that He will forgive all who come to Him. (See Isaiah 55:7.)

THE LESSON

1. JACOB'S FLIGHT
Genesis 27:41-28:5

What we think about, we talk about. Thinking and talking about things prepare us for doing them. That is why the Lord instructs us to think about things that are honest, just, pure, lovely, of good report. (See Philippians 4:8.)

The more Esau thought about Jacob's trickery, the angrier he became. Talking to his friends, he threatened, "After my father dies, I'm going to kill Jacob. He stole my birthright. He stole my father's blessing. He can't treat me like this and get away with it!"

One of the servants overheard Esau. He ran to Rebekah whispering, "Have you heard what Esau says? He will kill Jacob as soon as your husband dies!"

If only Rebekah had allowed God to direct her affairs, she would not have been in such a hard place. But again, instead of praying to God for guidance, she thought up another trick.

Sending for Jacob, she laid the scheme before him. "Esau hates you. He is plotting to kill you when your father dies. You must disappear for a while. Let Esau cool off and forget what you have done to him. Go to Haran. Spend some time with my family. When Esau gets over his anger, I will send for you."

"But what can I tell my father?" Jacob asked.

"Leave that to me, son. I'll think of something to fool him," his mother promised.

Soon Rebekah went to Isaac's tent with her scheme. "Isaac, my dear," she said smoothly, "I do not want Jacob to marry any of these heathen Canaanite girls. I am tired of the way they act. Esau's wives cause all kinds of problems. If Jacob marries a girl like these, life for me will not be worth living."

"Yes, yes. You are right, Rebekah," Isaac agreed.

Immediately the blind, aged Isaac called for Jacob. "My son," he said," your mother and I do not want you to marry one of the heathen girls who live here. My father Abraham sent his servant back to his homeland to get a wife for me. Now I want you to go there, too, to find a wife. May God Almighty bless you. I pray that He will give you many children. May you and your family become a great nation. May you own this land where we are now foreigners."

Rebekah's scheme had worked! Her husband was sending Jacob away–and blessing him too!

Show Illustration #5

With a wink, Jacob kissed his mother. "Good-bye," he said. And, turning his back on all that was familiar to him, Jacob began the long journey (500 miles) to Haran–alone. There was no camel train loaded with gifts like Eliezer (Abraham's servant) had. There were no servants to talk with. His only companion was fear–fear that Esau would overtake him and kill him. So he fled–looking behind him all the way.

As the sun began to sink in the sky at the end of the first day and the night closed in around him, Jacob felt very lonely. *Would he ever see home again?* he wondered. *What lay before? Was the blessing worth all that it was costing? What a dark night! What was that noise?*

The Bible does not tell us what he was thinking, but it could also have been something like this:

If only I had not lied to my father! If only I had not tricked Esau! Then I would not have had to flee for my life. I wonder if I shall ever be able to come back home. I wonder if I shall even see my parents again. Will my relatives accept me? Will they let me stay with them? Why did I steal Esau's birthright? Why did I trick my father to get his blessing? Why? Why?

It was too late to change those things.

I am nothing but a cheater. I hate myself for the way I have acted. Esau had a right to be angry. I am good for nothing.

Full of guilt, Jacob pillowed his head on a stone. There, alone, he fell into a troubled sleep.

2. JACOB'S VISION
Genesis 28:10-12

But there was Someone who saw Jacob–Someone who loved him and cared for him. Who? God. He knew Jacob was a liar, a trickster, a deceiver. Nevertheless He loved Jacob. And He had a plan for Jacob's life. That very night God Himself spoke to Jacob in a wonderful dream.

Show Illustration #6

In the dream, Jacob saw a ladder set up beside him on the earth. The top of the ladder reached up, up, up–right into Heaven! Jacob saw angels going up and down the ladder. What a marvelous sight that must have been!

Then he saw something even more wonderful. At the top of the ladder he saw the Lord! Oh, how ashamed Jacob was! He saw the Lord–the perfectly pure and good and holy One. And suddenly Jacob realized how full he was of pride and sin and wickedness. Jacob had sinned deliberately to get his own evil way. And his sin had separated him far from God. (See Isaiah 59:2.)

Looking into Heaven, Jacob thought to himself, *God is holy. He will not want to have anything to do with me. Oh, how wicked I am!*

3. GOD'S PROMISE
Genesis 28:13-15

But listen! In his dream God was speaking to him: "Jacob, I am the One who called your grandfather, Abraham, to this country. Your father, Isaac, worships Me. I am going to give you the same promise I gave them. I am going to bless you. I will give this land to you and your children. And I am going to bless all the families of the earth through you.

"You are lonely tonight, Jacob. You have done wrong. You are afraid and rightly so. You do not know what the future holds. But, Jacob, I am with you. Do not be afraid. I will keep you wherever you go. I will bring you back to this land again. I will not leave you until I have done all that I have promised."

How gracious and loving Almighty God is! Jacob did not deserve to see Him. He did not deserve the promises which God gave him. He did not deserve the assurance of God's presence. Jacob had all these promises simply because God loved him. It was as though God was saying, "Jacob, I am taking your hand. I will lead you from now on."

We have the same wicked, sinful nature Jacob had. We lie and deceive and take advantage of other people. Not one of us is righteous, no, not one! (See Romans 3:10.) We have all sinned. (See Romans 3:23.) Our sin separates us from God, the holy One (See Isaiah 59:2.), just as Jacob's sin separated him from God.

But God loves us. He loved us so much He sent His Son to die on the cross for our sins.

Show Illustration #7

The Lord Jesus Christ, by His death on the cross, is the ladder that leads us to God the Father in Heaven. (See John 14:6.) There is no other way to reach God.

Some people think: *I'll join a church and be baptized. Then I'll surely get to Heaven to live with God and His Son, Jesus Christ.* But church membership and baptism make a ladder that is too short to reach God. Believing that Jesus Christ is the Son of God and placing all your trust in Him is the *only* way to God. (See John 14:6.)

Others may think: *I am living a good life. I am kind to people. I help the sick and the poor. I have never killed anyone. I do not get angry. God will certainly receive me into His Heaven when I die.*

But that ladder is far too short. God says "All our righteousness (or good works) are as filthy rags" (Isaiah 64:6). We simply cannot be good enough.

Or maybe some are thinking: *I am too bad. God cannot save someone who has done the terrible things I have done. No one knows the evil thoughts I have. God cannot forgive me.*

But God says He sent His Son into the world to save sinners. (See Matthew 9:13; 1 Timothy 1:15.) You must realize you are a sinner. You must believe that Jesus Christ is the Son of God. You must believe He died for *your* sins. When you place all your trust in Him alone, you will be prepared for Heaven. When you receive Him as your Saviour, God will give you His new nature. (See 1 Corinthians 5:17.)

4. JACOB'S VOW
Genesis 28:18-22

Jacob woke up, startled by the heavenly vision he had just seen. He exclaimed, "The Lord is in this place and I didn't know it! This is truly the house of God and the entrance to Heaven!"

Show Illustration #8

The next morning Jacob set up the stone he had used as a pillow. He poured oil on it, marking the place where he had met God.

"I will never forget this spot. I am a guilty, hopeless sinner. But God has promised to go with me and bless me from now on. I shall call this place Bethel (house of God) and I shall never forget what happened here."

We wish Jacob would have said, "Dear God, I *know* You will do what You have promised. I will do whatever You command."

Instead, Jacob was full of doubts and fears. *Will I be able to find work so I can buy food and clothing?* he wondered. *Will I really get back home again?*

So he thought up another scheme. He would make a bargain with God. "My God," he said, "*if* You will really go with me and give me food to eat and clothes to wear, *if* You will bring me back home to my father's house, *then* You will be my God. And, *if* You do all this, *then* this pillar shall become a place to worship the living God. And dear God, I will give You a tenth of everything You give me."

Imagine trying to make a bargain with God! How much better it would have been if Jacob had simply trusted God to lead him, to protect him, to provide for him, and to direct him. He who had schemed to cheat his brother and deceive his father thought he could make a bargain with God.

But before you criticize Jacob too severely, think about yourself. Have you ever bargained with God? Have you said, "God, if you will do something good for me, then I will trust you? If You will get me out of this situation (*Teacher:* Name some difficulty which your students might face.), then I will receive the Lord Jesus Christ as my Saviour. And I shall love You for the rest of my life."

Have you ever said something like that? God does not accept those who try to bargain with Him. He will receive you when you receive His Son as Saviour. You may have been a schemer, a trickster, a deceiver, a liar. But if you are truly sorry for your sin and confess it to God, He will forgive your sin. If you believe that the Lord Jesus Christ is the Son of God and put all your trust in him, you will be born into the family of God. And you will receive a new nature–the nature of the Lord Jesus Christ Himself. Will you trust Him wholly?

Lesson 3
GOD'S DISCIPLINE

Scripture to be studied: Genesis 29:1–32:23

The *aim* of the lesson: To show that God uses difficulties in our lives to discipline us.

What your students should *know*: That God's discipline is good for us even though it is not pleasant.

What yours students should *feel*: Appreciation for God's discipline.

What your students should *do*: Submit to God and accept His discipline in their present circumstances.

Lesson outline (for the teacher's and students' notebooks):
1. Jacob deceived by Laban (Genesis 29:21-28).
2. Jacob tormented by family strife (Genesis 29:30–30:2).
3. Jacob misused by Laban (Genesis 30:25-35).
4. Jacob controlled by fear (Genesis 31:1-55).

The verse to be memorized:

Walk in the Spirit, and ye shall not fulfil the lust of the flesh. (Galatians 5:16)

> **NOTE TO THE TEACHER**
>
> Discipline is never pleasant. We naturally shrink from it. But God loves us. He uses difficulties and problems to make us obedient and useful. He wants us to be conformed to the image of His Son (Hebrews 12:5-7). Just as undisciplined children are displeasing to themselves and to others, so are undisciplined children of God.

THE LESSON

Were you disciplined recently? At home? At work? In school? (Encourage response.) How were you disciplined? What did you do to make it necessary? (Emphasize discipline is imperative in order to help us become obedient, useful and pleasing.) Parents discipline their children because they love them. If they did not love their sons and daughters, they would not care how naughty or disagreeable they are. Parents want others to love their children. They know children must respect others, must listen to those in authority, and must be considerate of others.

God disciplines the people He loves. (See Hebrews 12:5-6.) He does not use a switch to beat His children. But He brings problems into their lives. Problems force them to think about Him and pray for His help.

God loved Jacob very much. But, Jacob was so busy doing things his own way that he did not take time to ask God to help him. Jacob treated his father and brother so unkindly that he was forced to leave home and flee for his life.

If Jacob was to become the right kind of person, God would have to discipline him. Did He? Listen carefully!

1. JACOB DECEIVED BY LABAN
Genesis 29:21-28

Jacob was afraid. His thoughts were filled with his dream of the night before. God Himself had opened up Heaven. He had promised Jacob some marvelous blessings. Instead of thanking God for His goodness, Jacob had proudly offered God a bargain. He actually told God that *if* He (God) would keep His promises, *then* he (Jacob) would do good things for God. Imagine that! So proud Jacob the deceiver, the liar, the trickster, the bargainer, went on his lonely way.

After several weeks of walking, Jacob saw some shepherds with their flocks. "Where are you from?" he asked.

"We are from Haran," they answered.

"Do you know a man named Laban in Haran?" Jacob continued.

"Yes, we know him. Look! There is his daughter, Rachel, coming with her father's sheep, " they replied.

When Jacob saw Rachel, he immediately fell in love with her–and kissed her! Rachel was surprised to be greeted as a family member.

Weeping loudly, Jacob explained, "Rachel, your father is my mother's brother. I have come a long distance to meet you and your family."

Leaving the flocks, Rachel ran home.

"Father!" she called breathlessly. "Guess whom I met at the well? Aunt Rebekah's son, Jacob. He has come all the way from Canaan to meet us."

Laban rushed to the well, embraced Jacob, and invited him to come to his house.

Jacob felt right at home immediately and began to work for his uncle. A month later Laban said, "Jacob, you are a good worker. I am glad for your help. Even though you are my nephew, I do not expect you to work for nothing. What would you like in exchange for your labor?"

"Uncle Laban, I love your daughter Rachel. I will be happy to work for seven years if you will give her to me for my wife," Jacob answered.

"I would rather give her to you than to anyone else, Jacob. It is a bargain. You work seven years. Then Rachel shall be your wife," Laban promised.

Those years slipped by quickly. Jacob worked hard. Then one day he said, "Uncle Laban, I have kept my part of the bargain. I have worked seven years for you. Now it is time for you to give me Rachel to be my wife."

"Yes, Jacob, you have served me well. I will plan the wedding feast. You shall have my daughter as your wife," promised Laban.

What a happy, festive time they had! Laban prepared a big feast. Everyone was happy. In the evening, Laban led his daughter to Jacob's tent. She had a heavy veil over her face since that was their custom.

Jacob whispered to his bride, "I have worked seven years for this day, my beloved Rachel. Now we can begin our lives together."

Show Illustration #9

But when the sun came up the next morning, and the veil was removed from his bride's face, Jacob was horrified! He rushed out of the tent, shouting to Laban, "What have you done to me? You did not give me Rachel as you had promised. You gave me Leah, her older sister! How could you do this to me? I do not love Leah! I do not want her for my wife! I love Rachel. I worked for Rachel. You have deceived me. You broke your promise!"

Laban had treated Jacob exactly as Jacob had treated his brother seven years before. God was teaching Jacob that "whatever a man sows, that he also reaps" (Galatians 6:7). God was disciplining Jacob for his own deceit. Now Jacob knew what it felt like to be tricked by someone.

"There, there, Jacob, don't be upset," Laban answered. "According to the custom of our country, I could not let Rachel get married before her older sister was married. You wanted Rachel. You will have her. After the wedding celebration is over next week, I will give you Rachel. But you must work seven more years for her," Laban added smugly. He was showing his sinful nature now! He had gotten his own way. But, oh, what it cost Jacob!

Jacob loved Rachel so much that he agreed to work another seven years for her.

2. JACOB TORMENTED BY FAMILY STRIFE
Genesis 29:30-30:2

Now Jacob really had a problem. He had two wives instead of one! And he loved only Rachel. In fact, he hated Leah. This made Leah jealous of Rachel. Instead of peace and happiness at home, there were arguing, fighting, weeping, and heartache.

Why do I have all these problems? Jacob wondered.

God might well have said, "Jacob, remember all the heartache you caused in your own family! You tricked your brother. You deceived your blind, aged father. Remember? You have made others suffer. Now I am disciplining you with suffering."

In time, God gave Leah a baby boy. But still Jacob did not love her. Three more boys were born to Jacob and Leah. But Jacob loved only Rachel.

Show Illustration #10

Rachel wanted a baby and became jealous of Leah. She often scolded Jacob. Day after day there was trouble in Jacob's home. He was reaping what he had sown.

3. JACOB MISUSED BY LABAN
Genesis 30:25-35

While God was teaching Jacob some hard lessons, He was also blessing him. He gave Jacob strong, healthy sons. Even Laban was becoming wealthy because of Jacob. (See Genesis 30:27.)

One day Jacob said to his Uncle Laban, "I want to take my wives and children back to my own country. I have served you well for 14 years. Now I want to go home."

"Please do not leave me, Jacob," Laban begged. "It is because of you that the Lord has blessed me. Tell me how much pay you want. I will give you whatever you ask."

"Laban, you know that when I came you didn't have very much. I have worked hard for you. Now you are wealthy. The Lord has blessed you because of me. Even so, you have changed your agreements ten times, reducing my wages. It is time for me to take care of my own family and get some animals for myself."

"Do not leave, Jacob. Tell me what you want. I will give you whatever you ask," Laban promised.

"I will stay and work for you, Laban, if you will give me all the spotted, striped and brown animals in the flocks. Each time new animals are born, if they are spotted, striped or brown, they will be mine. The others will be yours.

Show Illustration #11

Laban thought to himself, *That is not a hard bargain. I will simply separate all the spotted, striped and brown ones from the rest of the flock right now. Then there will not be any more born like that.*

That's just what Laban did. He thought he had tricked Jacob again. But this time God showed Laban that he could not get by with his scheme. God caused many of

– 23 –

the baby sheep, goats and cattle to be born brown or with spots or stripes. Soon Jacob had more animals (and stronger ones!) than Laban. How angry Laban became! Because of his sin nature, Laban selfishly thought only of himself.

4. JACOB CONTROLLED BY FEAR
Genesis 31:1-55

One day Jacob heard Laban's sons complaining. "Jacob is getting wealthy at our father's expense. That's not right," they said.

Jacob observed that Laban was not friendly toward him any more. Laban was jealous because God was blessing Jacob.

One night God spoke to Jacob. "Go back to your homeland and your relatives," He commanded. "I will be with you."

Without delay, Jacob talked secretly with Rachel and Leah. "I am afraid of your father," he whispered. "God has told me to get out of this land and return to my country. So we are going. We will sneak away quietly while your father is with his sheep."

So, instead of depending upon God, Jacob schemed to slip away unnoticed. His sinful nature was in control. Away he went, looking back over his shoulder all the way.

When Laban heard that Jacob was gone, he was furious. "I shall catch up with him! I'll show him he cannot treat me this way!" he threatened. For seven days he and his men raced after Jacob.

One night in a dream God said, "Laban! Do not touch Jacob!"

Show Illustration #12

When Laban caught up with Jacob, he did not hurt him. Sadly he kissed his daughters and grandchildren goodbye.

Then Jacob went on his way. Day after day the camel caravan moved slowly toward his homeland. It had been twenty years since he had seen his family. Now Jacob felt another fear mounting in his heart. *Will Esau still be angry with me?* he wondered. *Will he try to kill me when we meet? I deceived him. I stole his blessing. I know now how he feels. I did not like it when Laban tricked me. But I forgave Laban. Will Esau forgive me?*

Jacob was reaping fear from the trickery and lies which he had sown. He learned these past years that those who do wrong have many troubles (See Proverbs 13:15.). There had been many disappointments. There was unhappiness between his wives. Now he wasn't sure he would be received by his own brother! Then he saw Esau. What happened? We will learn that in our next lesson.

Are you obeying God today? Are you trusting Him to care for you? Or are you scheming to make things work for your good? If you depend upon yourself, your tricks and your lies, instead of trusting in God, He will discipline you. Maybe you are experiencing problems, disappointments, discouragements, difficulties. These may be God's ways of teaching you to trust Him alone.

Ask God to show you what He is teaching you. If you are willing to obey and trust Him only, will you tell Him right now?

Lesson 4
GOD GAINS CONTROL OF JACOB'S LIFE

NOTE TO THE TEACHER

When we trusted Christ as Saviour, we became new creations (2 Corinthians 5:17). Like Paul, we can say "Christ liveth in me" (Galatians 2:20). By nature we are children of wrath. And this nature produces all kinds of sinful acts. (See Ephesians 2:3.) Sometimes the sin nature is referred to as the *flesh*. (See Romans 7:18.) It has the same meaning in our memory verse for this series. The old nature of the flesh is that capacity which we have to serve and please self. The old nature leaves God out. In the Christian the flesh is that same capacity to leave God out of his life and actions. (*Teacher:* For a good explanation of the old and new natures read chapter four of *Balancing the Christian Life* by Dr. Charles C. Ryrie, published by Moody Press, Chicago, IL. This is an excellent volume and every teacher should have it.)

The unsaved man has only one capacity. But the Christian has two, This means that the unsaved person serves sin and self leaving God out of his life. The believer may serve God and, as long as he is in a human body, he may also choose to leave God out and live according to the old nature.

The new nature comes from God Himself. (See 2 Peter 1:4; Ephesians 41;22-25; Galatians 5:17, 25; and Romans 7:15-25; 8:6.)

God patiently deals with us (2 Peter 3:9) to make us what He wants us to become (1 Peter 5:10). We may think we are strong and can live our own lives. But we fail. Without Christ we can do nothing. With Christ we can do all things through Him who gives us strength (Philippians 4:13). When these truths are our daily experience, we live a life of blessing.

Scripture to be studied: Genesis 32, 33, 35

The *aim* of the lesson: To show that believers are victorious only when they allow the Spirit of God to rule their lives.

What your students should *know*: Our human natures are weak and helpless. But God wants to strengthen us to live for Him.

What your students should *feel*: That without Christ's strength, we can do nothing.

What your students should *do*: Submit to the Lord and allow Him to control their lives.

Lesson outline (for the teacher's and students' notebooks):

1. Jacob continues to scheme (Genesis 32:2-21).
2. God wrestles with Jacob (Genesis 32:24-25).
3. Jacob submits to God (Genesis 32:26-30).
4. Jacob worships God (Genesis 33:18-20).

The verse to be memorized:

Walk in the Spirit, and ye shall not fulfil the lust of the flesh. (Galatians 5:16)

THE LESSON
1. JACOB CONTINUES TO SCHEME
Genesis 32:2-21

The closer Jacob came to home, the more afraid he became. Why was he so fearful? (Review briefly the events of Jacob's life. Emphasize that sin makes us fearful.) Do you think Jacob should have been frightened? (Emphasize Jacob's lack of faith and trust in God. If Jacob had believed God, he would have known that Esau could not harm him.)

God wanted Jacob to realize that He (God) could protect him. So God caused Jacob to see a multitude of angels around him. What a glorious sight!

But as usual, Jacob's old nature was active. He thought he had to help God carry out His plans. Calling some of his servants, Jacob gave them orders; "Go to my brother Esau! Give him my greeting. Explain that I have been living with Uncle Laban. Now I am returning with many animals and servants. Tell him, too, that I hope he will be friendly."

Jacob's men obeyed. Soon they returned, exclaiming, "We met your brother, Esau! We never did have a chance to give him your message! He is coming to meet you. And he has 400 men with him!"

Jacob was terrified. *Esau is planning to kill me! He is coming with 400 men!* Forgetting about the angels of God, he decided to do something quickly.

We would like to say, "Jacob, Jacob! God commanded you to return home. He promised to protect you. He said He would give you many descendants (children, grandchildren, great-grandchildren). How could God keep His promises if Esau should kill you and your family? Remember! The angels of God are with you!"

But Jacob was too busy making plans to protect his family and flocks. He had no time to think about God.

Show Illustration #13

Commanding his servants, Jacob shouted, "Divide the men, women, and children into two groups. Put half the animals with one group. The other half goes with the second group. Hurry!" Everyone obediently sprang into action.

Jacob reasoned to himself, *If Esau kills one group maybe the second will be able to escape.*

After arranging everything, Jacob prayed: "Dear Lord, I need Your help. Years ago when I left home, I owned nothing but my shepherd's staff. You have blessed me with sons, servants and animals. Now please do not allow Esau to kill us. I am afraid of him. Remember! You promised to give me a huge family–too many to be numbered."

Jacob ended his prayer to God. Then he thought up his own plan for making peace with Esau. *I will send a present to Esau,* he decided. *Maybe then he will be friendly to us.*

So Jacob chose more than 500 animals and divided them into groups. He put a servant at the head of each group. Then he gave instructions: "When you meet my brother, Esau, he will ask, 'Who are you? Where are you going? To whom do these animals belong?' Tell him, 'These belong to your servant, Jacob. They are presents for you. He is coming right behind us.'"

Jacob thought: *When Esau sees such a large gift, he may be pleased. Then perhaps he will not be angry with me.*

2. GOD WRESTLES WITH JACOB
Genesis 32:24-25

After everything was on its way, Jacob settled down for the night–alone. He tried to sleep but could not. All kinds of thoughts raced through his mind. *Will Esau accept my gifts? Will he be friendly? Or will he kill me and my family?*

Suddenly, a hand grabbed him!

Show Illustration #14

Jacob seized the man and a wrestling match began.

How strong he is! Jacob thought. He strained every muscle trying not to be pinned to the ground.

The Stranger would not give up. Jacob would not give up. The struggle continued fiercely.

Jacob wondered, *Who is this Wrestler? What strength He has! I cannot let Him defeat me!* Jacob did not know it, but he was actually wrestling with God. Imagine that! Why would God wrestle with Jacob? Because God knew there was only one way to make Jacob useful. Jacob had to learn not to trust in his own plans and schemes. He had to see his weaknesses. And he had to understand that God is the strong, faithful One.

God wanted Jacob to understand that it was impossible to change Esau's heart with gifts. God alone, through His power, could change Esau. God alone could make him friendly toward Jacob. God alone could get Jacob safely home.

The struggle continued all night. Jacob was worn out but he would not give up.

God touched Jacob's hip and knocked it out of joint.

3. JACOB SUBMITS TO GOD
Genesis 32:26-30

In terrible pain, Jacob fell to the ground helpless. His strength was gone. The bout was over. Jacob was defeated. He knew now that it was God who had wrestled with Him. So Jacob clung to the Wrestler.

"Let me go," God said. "It is daybreak."

"No, No!" Jacob exclaimed. "I will not let You go until You bless me."

That is exactly what God wanted to do. All these years Jacob had refused God's blessings. Always Jacob had been choosing his own way, leaving God out of things. Now Jacob could do nothing. He was willing to let God choose for him.

"What is your name?" God asked. God knew Jacob's name, of course. But He wanted Jacob to see that he had been just what his name means – a deceiver, trickster, schemer. Now Jacob saw himself as God saw him. There was nothing good in Jacob. There was nothing in Jacob that could please God.

"I am going to change your name," God said. "You will not be Jacob anymore. Your name is Israel. Instead of being known as a deceiver and a trickster, you will be a prince with God. You have tried to direct your own life. You have left Me out and have failed. Now, if you will let Me, I am going to control your life. And you will be blessed."

God touched Jacob and made him physically helpless. Then Jacob was willing to give his life to the Lord.

From that night on, Jacob limped. This always reminded him that he must depend on the Spirit of God alone in every experience of life.

God wants us to see ourselves as He sees us. How does He see you and me? He does not see one good thing in us. (See Romans 7:18.) Nothing that we do is good in God's sight. (See Romans 3:12.) He sees us making our own plans and going our own way. This does not please Him. (See Romans 8:8.)

Sometimes God must wrestle with us by bringing difficulties and problems into our lives. Then we can see ourselves as He sees us – weak and helpless. He wants us to turn our lives over to him completely. He wants us to let Him guide our plans. He wants us to honor Him.

He wants us to admit that "without Him we can do nothing" (John 15:5). But we can do all things through Christ who gives us strength (Philippians 4:13).

When you allow the Holy Spirit of God to control your life, you need not fear anyone or anything, for when you live and walk in the Spirit you will not carry out your own selfish desires. (*Teacher:* Have students quote the memory verse.) When you have decisions to make or fears to overcome, talk to God about them and ask Him to take charge. And He will! Just trust *Him!*

Show Illustration #15

Limping Jacob, controlled by the Spirit of God, was ready to meet Esau without fear. And God had prepared Esau. He did not try to kill Jacob. Instead he embraced him and kissed him. He asked all about Jacob's family.

After a friendly visit, Esau returned to his home. And Jacob set up the tents for his family so they could rest from their long journey.

4. JACOB WORSHIPS GOD
Genesis 33:18-20

Show Illustration #16

For the first time in 20 years, Jacob built an altar and worshiped God. The Bible has not recorded Jacob's prayer, but it could have been something like this:

"O God of my father Abraham, my father Isaac, and my God. I thank you for bringing me back to my country as you promised. I thank You for making Esau friendly toward me. I am sorry I was afraid and did not trust You. I have tried to run my own life and I have failed miserably.

"Take charge of my life, dear God. Show me how to live today. Help me to make right decisions. I want to know Your will and obey it."

Like Jacob, your old sinful nature will always fail. But when the Lord Jesus Christ is your Saviour, the Spirit of God lives inside you. And that new nature from Him will give you victory over sin. God's Spirit wants your old sinful nature defeated. Will you allow God to rule your life? Will you ask Him to help you choose His way? Will you allow your new nature to be in control? Will you talk to God about it right now? (Teacher: Allow time for decisions and prayer. Whatever decisions your students make should be recorded in their notebooks along with the date.)